SONIC™
THE HEDGEHOG

THE OFFICIAL
COLOR BY STICKER
BOOK

INSIGHT
EDITIONS

SAN RAFAEL · LOS ANGELES · LONDON

HOW TO DO IT

Ready to create your own colorful pictures from the world of Sonic the Hedgehog? It's easy!

1. Choose which picture you want to bring to life. You can start with any page you want! The pages are easy to remove from the book, so you don't have to flip back and forth.

2. Find the sticker page that matches the picture you've chosen. There's a small picture on each sticker page to help you find the right stickers.

3. Each sticker has a number. Just peel off the sticker and place it in the spot on the picture that has the same number! You can put the stickers in place in any order you want.

INSIGHT
EDITIONS

Insight Editions
PO Box 3088
San Rafael, CA 94912

www.insighteditions.com

f Find us on Facebook: www.facebook.com/InsightEditions

ISBN: 978-1-64722-901-6

Publisher: Raoul Goff
VP of Licensing and Partnerships: Vanessa Lopez
VP of Creative: Chrissy Kwasnik
VP of Manufacturing: Alix Nicholaeff
VP, Editorial Director: Vicki Jaeger
Senior Designer: Judy Wiatrek Trum
Editor: Rick Chillot
Production Associate: Tiffani Patterson

Illustrations by Mario Gushiken

Sonic

Tails

Amy

Dr. Eggman

Super Sonic

Knuckles

Shadow

Omega

**Metal
Sonic**

Rouge

Sonic

Tails

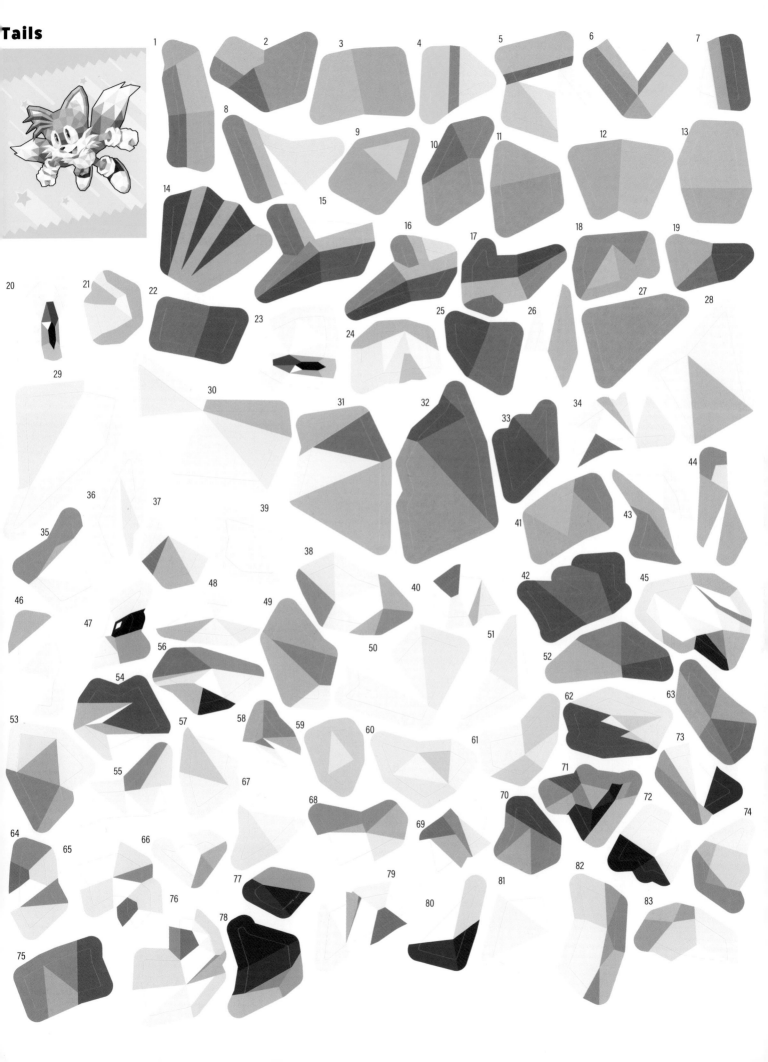

Amy

Dr. Eggman

Super Sonic

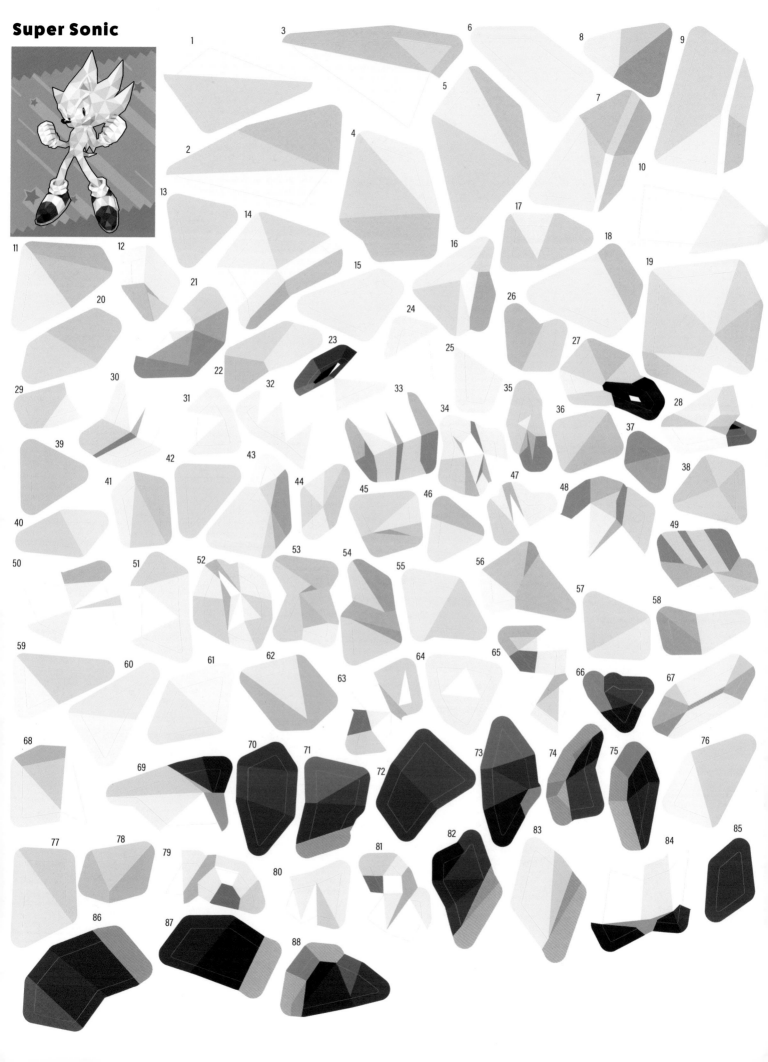

Knuckles

Shadow

Omega

Metal Sonic

Rouge

Sonic